P9-CMQ-564

A Special Gift

For

_____

From

_____

Date

_____

Message

_____

_____

Inspiration for Living

HELEN STEINER RICE

TINY TREASURE-SERIES

R Fleming H. Revell

INSPIRATION FOR LIVING

Where there is love
The heart is light,
Where there is love
The day is bright.

Let me hear in the morning of
thy steadfast love, for in thee
I put my trust.
Teach me the way I should go,
for to thee I lift up my soul.

Psalm: 143:8

Today there will be no
heaviness of heart and no
darkness prevailing because love
abounds.

When trouble surrounds you
And no one understands,
Try placing your cares
In God's open hands.

*Into your hands I commend
my spirit ...*
Psalm 31:5

Today concentrate on being
optimistic, not pessimistic.

When everything is quiet
And we're lost in meditation,
Our soul is then preparing
For a deeper dedication.

*Oh, how I love thy law! It is my
meditation all the day.*

Psalm 119:97

Today close out the noise of
everyday living and listen to
that hushed voice deep within.
Meditate in silence.

May this land remain forever
The proud and upright
symbol of
A free and mighty nation
Built on faith and truth and
love!

Righteousness exalts a nation,
but sin is a reproach to
any people.
Proverbs 14:34

Today pray for inspiration and
guidance for the leaders of our
city, state, nation.

There's a lot of comfort
in the thought
That sorrow, grief, and woe
Are sent into our lives sometimes
To help our souls to grow.

*In the fear of the Lord is strong
confidence: and his children
shall have a place of refuge.*
Proverbs 14:26 KJV

Today accept your personal
disappointments uncomplainingly.
Showers are needed for flowers
to grow and some tears are
necessary in our lives to
promote our inner growth.

Thank you, God, for brushing
The dark clouds from my mind
And leaving only sunshine
And joy of heart behind.

*The heart knows its own
bitterness, and no stranger
shares its joy.*
Proverbs 14:10

Today display an unselfish
heart.

Teach me, dear God,
To not rush ahead,
But to pray for Your guidance
And to trust You instead.

*Good sense makes a man slow to
anger, and it is his glory to
overlook an offence.*
Proverbs 19:11

Today do not worry. Worry is
like riding a carousel: you keep
going around, but you get
nowhere.

On the wings of prayer
Our burdens take flight –
Our load of care
Becomes bearably light.

*Cast your burden upon the Lord,
and He will sustain you; He will
never allow the righteous
to be shaken.*

Psalm: 55:22 NAS

Today with prayer the rough
and trying times can be made
bearable.

Our Father up in heaven
Is very much aware
Of our failures and
shortcomings,
And the burdens that we bear.

My flesh and my heart may fail,
but God is the strength of my
heart and my portion for ever.
Psalm: 73:26

Today implore God to mend
your broken heart, to tie it back
together with His loving hands.

Often we stand at
life's crossroads
And view what we think
is the end,
But God has a much
bigger vision
And He tells us it's
only a bend.

*Make me to know thy ways, O
Lord; teach me thy paths.*
Psalm 25:4

Today avoid any sign
of self-pity.

Never dread tomorrow
Or what the future brings,
Just pray for strength
and courage
And trust God in all things.

*In everything you do, put God
first, and he will direct you and
crown your efforts with success.*
Proverbs 3:6 TLB

Today acknowledge your
limitations and your reliance
upon God, remembering that He
will supply the necessary
strength to try and try again.
With each day you can begin
anew.

The more you love,
the more you'll find
That life is good and
friends are kind,
And only what we give away
Enriches us from day to day.

*What is desired in a
man is loyalty.*
Proverbs 19:22

Today maintain a spirit of
cooperation, harmony, fidelity,
and allegiance.

May I never give way to
self-pity and sorrow,
May I always be sure of
a better tomorrow,
May I stand undaunted
come what may,
Secure in the knowledge
I have only to pray.

*Gracious is the Lord, and
righteous; yea, our God is
merciful. The Lord preserveth
the simple: I was brought low,
and he helped me.*
Psalm 116:5, 6 KJV

Today do not quit – carry on.
Look ahead, not back.
Regret is futile.

May He who sends
the raindrops
And makes the sunshine, too,
Look down and bless you richly
And be very near to you!

*Thou hast fixed all the bounds of
the earth; thou hast made
summer and winter.*

Psalm 74:17

Today let the only person you
try to impress be God.

Make us more aware,
dear God,
Of little daily graces
That come to us with
sweet surprise
From never-dreamed-of places.

My God, in you I trust.
Psalm 25:2 NAB

Today ask yourself: "What lesson can be learned from the experience of this day?"

Little prayers for little things
Fly heavenward on little wings
And no prayer is too
great or small
To ask God who hears them all.

Keep me as the apple of the eye;
hide me in the shadow
of thy wings …
Psalm 17:8

Today, this very morning, kneel
to meet and greet the Lord.
No one is ever greater in stature
than when kneeling in
prayer to God.

Life is a mixture of
Sunshine and rain,
Teardrops and laughter,
Pleasure and pain.

Even in laughter the heart is
sad, and the end of joy is grief.
Proverbs 14:13

Today accept disappointments
as well as joys… even a
beautiful rose has a few thorns.

True communication
Is reached through God alone,
To Him the thoughts
we cannot express
Are understood and known.

*How precious to me are thy
thoughts, O God! How vast is
the sum of them!*
Psalm 139:17

Today be faithful in the small
things and you can't help but be
faithful in the large.

Let me serve You every day
And feel You near me
when I pray…
Hear my prayer,
dear God above,
And make me worthy
of Your love!

Be exalted above the heavens,
O God; Let Thy glory be
above all the earth!
Psalm 57:5 NAS

Today help to clothe God's
sheep and feed His lambs.

It's amazing and incredible,
But it's as true as it can be,
God loves and understands
us all,
And that means you and me!

*My son, do not despise the
Lord's discipline or be weary
of his reproof, for the Lord
reproves him whom he loves, as
a father the son in whom
he delights.*
Proverbs 3:11, 12

Today respect everyone – even
those who appear different from
you; for we are all created by the
same Father.

Into our lives come many things
to break the dull routine,
Things we had not planned
or that happen unforeseen…
An unsought word of kindness,
a compliment or two
Sets the eyes to gleaming –
like crystal drops of dew.

*Good news from far away is
like cold water to the thirsty.*
Proverbs 25:25 TLB

Today open the window of your
heart and let your light and love
shine through. The happiness
you share with others will
circulate back to you.

In this wavering world
of unbelief
We are filled with doubt
and questioning fear –
Oh, give us faith
in things unseen
So we may feel Thy
presence near.

Thy way was through the sea,
thy path through the great
waters; yet thy footprints
were unseen.
Psalm: 77:19

Today work on spiritual
awareness.

In this troubled world
it's refreshing to find
Someone who still takes
the time to be kind.
Someone who's ready by
thought, word, or deed
To reach out a hand in
the hour of need.

*He who is kind to the poor lends
to the Lord, and he will reward
him for what he has done.*
Proverbs 19:17 NIV

Today give time to the sick,
needy, and homeless, for if you
ignore them, you ignore God.

If you practice kindness
In all you say and do,
The Lord will wrap His kindness
Around your heart and you..

He who pursues righteousness
and kindness will find life
and honour.
Proverbs 21:21

Today be a source of
encouragement.

God's love is like a fortress
And we seek protection there
When the waves of tribulation
Seem to drown us in despair!

*Then they cried to the Lord in
their trouble, and he delivered
them from their distress; he
made the storm be still, and the
waves of the sea were hushed.*
Psalm 107:28, 29

Today remember that with only
one stroke, a minus (–)
can be turned into a plus (+).

God bless our nation
And keep us safe and free,
Safe from all our enemies
Wherever they may be.

*Blessed is the nation whose
God is the Lord.*

Psalm 33:12 TLB

Today pray for solutions to
national and international
problems.

Faith makes it wholly possible
To quietly endure
The violent world around us –
For in God we are secure.

*Therefore my heart is glad, and
my soul rejoices; my body also
dwells secure.*

Psalm 16:9

Today trust in God with
deepened conviction. Ask Him
to stay close to you.

Every happy happening
And every lucky break
Are little gifts from God above
That are ours to freely take.

Sing to the Lord, bless his name;
tell of his salvation from
day to day.

Psalm 96:2

Today repeat often,
"I am someone special, a unique
individual created by
God and filled with potential."

Deal only with the present,
Never step into tomorrow,
For God asks us just
to trust Him
And to never borrow sorrow.

*For our heart rejoices in Him,
because we trust in
His holy name.*
Psalm 33:21 NAS

Today be flexible, adaptable,
and receptive.

A better world for all mankind
Where we are safe and free
Must start not with
our fellowmen
But within the heart of "me".

From heaven the Lord looks
down and sees all mankind …
Psalm 33:13 NIV

Today live by the rule that
"peace in the world begins with
me and within me".

Be glad that you've walked
With courage each day,
Be glad you've had strength
For each step of the way.

*Keep steady my steps according
to thy promise ...*
Psalm 119:133

Today let each step you take
bring you closer to walking as
Jesus walked.

A word of understanding
Spoken in an hour of trial
Is an unexpected miracle
That makes life more
worthwhile.

My mouth shall speak wisdom;
the meditation of my heart shall
be understanding.

Psalm 49:3

Today speak words of
compassion. You can help to
soften the sorrow of a friend.

When the door to our heart
Is open wide,
The sunshine of love
Will come inside.

*Probe me, O God, and know my
heart; try me and know my
thoughts!*
Psalm 139:23 NAB

Today practice inward charm. It
cultivates love. Love radiates
from within.

When I just keep quiet
And think only thoughts
of peace
And if I abide in stillness,
My restless murmurings cease.

*Be still, and know
that I am God ...*
Psalm: 46:10

Today accept yourself with
loving-kindness. Be considerate
of yourself. Take time to think
quietly and peacefully and enjoy
the serenity that emerges.

There's no problem too big
And no question too small,
Just ask God in faith
And He'll answer them all.

Commit your work to the Lord,
and your plans will be
established.
Proverbs 16:3

Today rejoice in the knowledge
that God listens to each and
every prayer, irrespective of the
magnitude of the request.

Thank You, God, for sending
A happy thought my way
To blot out my depression
On a disappointing day.

*Anxious hearts are very heavy
but a word of encouragement
does wonders!*
Proverbs 12:25 TLB

Today you may not see any
sunbeams, but remember, the
sun is still there.

Thank You, God,
for little things
That often come our way –
The things we take for granted
But don't mention
when we pray.

*Better is a little with
righteousness than great
revenues with injustice.*
Proverbs 16:8

Today thank God for your
many blessings.

So we may know God better
And feel His quiet power,
Let us daily keep in silence
A meditation hour.

*May the words of my mouth and
the meditation of my heart be
pleasing in your sight, O Lord,
my Rock and my Redeemer.*

Psalm 19:14 NIV

Today enrich your life. Take
time to become better
acquainted with God.

Peace begins within our
own being
Where God resides beyond
our seeing,
And peace is one thing
you'll never find
When you are at war in
your own heart and mind.

*For my brethren and
companions' sake I will say,
"Peace be within you!"*
Psalm 122:8

Today peace will be with you
when you invite God to
dwell within.

Oh, God,
who made the summer
And warmed the earth
with beauty,
Warm our hearts with gratitude
And devotion to our duty.

*Enter his gates with
thanksgiving, and his courts
with praise! Give thanks to him,
bless his name!*

Psalm 100:4

Today grow in gratitude.

The more you give,
The more you get –
The more you laugh,
The less you fret!

*The meek shall possess the land,
and delight themselves in
abundant prosperity.*
Psalm 37:11

Today laugh at your mistakes.

Make us conscious that Your
love comes in many ways
Not always just as happiness or
bright and shining days.
Often You send trouble and we
foolishly reject it
Not realising that it is Your will
and we should joyously accept it.

*He who spares his rod hates his
son, but he who loves him
disciplines him diligently.*

Proverbs 13:24 NAS

Today keep in mind that, even
during difficult times, God is
transmitting His love and
sending needed discipline into
your life.

Lord, don't let me stumble,
Don't let me fall and quit,
Lord, please help me
find my job
And help me shoulder it.

*Keep sound wisdom and
discretion... Then you walk on
your way securely and your foot
will not stumble.*
Proverbs 3:21, 23

Today practice perseverance.

Like a soaring eagle
You too can rise above
The storms of life around you
On the wings of prayer and love.

*O God, have pity, for I am
trusting you! I will hide beneath
the shadow of your wings until
this storm is past.*

Psalm 57:1 TLB

Today a prayer and an
expression of love can lift a
depressed spirit.

Let us be content to solve
Our problems, one by one,
Asking nothing of
tomorrow, except
"Thy will be done."

Do not boast about tomorrow,
for you do not know what a day
may bring forth.
Proverbs 27:1

Today concentrate on one
problem at a time.

It's not the things that can
be bought
That are life's richest treasure,
It's just the little heart gifts
That money cannot measure.

*Better is little with the fear of the
Lord than great treasure and
trouble therewith.*
Proverbs 15:16 KJV

Today appreciate your
treasures: faith, family, and
friends are the most valuable and
yet are unavailable for purchase.

I sometimes think that friendliness
Is like a cheerful song…
It makes the good days better,
And it helps when things go
wrong.

*The Lord is my strength and my
shield; in him my heart trusts; so
I am helped, and my heart
exalts, and with my song I give
thanks to him.*

Psalm 28:7

Today a song in the heart will
put a smile on the face and so
will calling on a friend.

Help all people everywhere
Who must often dwell apart
To know that they're together
In the haven of the heart!

*Glorify the Lord with me; let us
exalt his name together.*

Psalm 34:3 NIV

Today, even though loved ones
are miles away, remember them
with prayers and fond
recollections.

God's love is like an island
In life's ocean vast and wide –
A peaceful, quiet shelter
From the restless, rising tide!

I would haste to find me a
shelter from the raging wind
and tempest.
Psalm: 55:8

Today let God's love and His
everlasting arms offer security
and shelter.

God knows no strangers,
He loves us all,
The poor, the rich
The great, the small!

*Rich and poor have a common
bond; the LORD is the maker
of them all.*

Proverbs 22:2 NAB

Today introduce someone to
God. God loves to make
new friends.

Faith is a mover of mountains,
And there's nothing
that God cannot do,
So start out today with faith in
your heart and climb till your
dream comes true!

*Lord, thou hast been our
dwelling place in all
generations.*

Psalm 90:1

Today avoid making mountains
out of molehills.

Give us reassurance
When everything goes wrong
So our faith remains unfaltering
And our hope and
courage strong.

*Be strong, and let your heart
take courage, all you who wait
for the Lord!*

Psalm 31:24

Today be a living mirror –
reflect your faith in God

Faith to endure
whatever comes
Is born of sorrow and trials,
And strengthened by
daily discipline
And nurtured by self-denials.

I weep with grief; my heart is
heavy with sorrow; encourage
and cheer me with your words.
Psalm 119:28 *TLB*

Today learn from your
experiences and errors of
yesterday.

Every home
Is specially blessed
When God becomes
A daily guest.

*Every day I will bless thee,
and praise thy name for
ever and ever*

Psalm 145:2

Today and every day put out
the welcome mat for Jesus.
Invite Him to enter each heart
and home.

Do what you do
With a will and a smile
And whatever you do
Will be twice as worthwhile.

I delight to do thy will, O my
God: yea, thy law is within
my heart.
Psalm 40:8 KJV

Today keep hope in your life
and a smile on your face.

Cheerful thoughts like
sunbeams
Lighten up the darkest fears
For when the heart is happy
There's just no time for tears.

*A glad heart makes a cheerful
countenance, but by sorrow of
heart the spirit is broken.*
Proverbs 15:13

Today fill an emptiness in
someone's life rather than
adding to the loneliness.

Among the great and
glorious gifts
Our heavenly Father sends
Is the gift of understanding
That we find in loving friends.

*A friend loves at all times, and a
brother is born for adversity.*
Proverbs 17:17

Today locate Jesus in the
people you meet and in
everyday happenings.

When you're feeling downcast,
Seek God in meditation,
For a little talk with Jesus
Is unfailing medication.

*I shall delight in Thy
commandments, which I love ...
and I will meditate on
Thy statutes.*
Psalm 119:47, 48 NAS

Today remind yourself that a
cheerful disposition is an
outward sign of an inward state.

The way we use adversity
Is strictly our own choice,
For in God's hands adversity
Can make the heart rejoice.

I will rejoice and be glad for thy
steadfast love, because thou hast
seen my affliction, thou
has taken heed of my
adversities.

Psalm 31:7

Today demonstrate
dependability, for it is equally as
important as your ability.

Time cannot be halted
In its swift and endless flight
For age is sure to follow youth
Like day comes after night.

Do not cast me away when I am
old; do not forsake me when my
strength is gone.

Psalm 71:9 NIV

Today plan for the future since
you are the architect of your
own life.

Love has all the qualities
Of an eternal light
That keeps the garments of
the soul
Clean and pure and bright.

*The unfolding of thy words gives
light; it imparts understanding
to the simple … Turn to me and
be gracious to me, as is thy wont
toward those who love
thy name.*

Psalm: 119:130, 132

Today pattern your life after a
candle – radiate light to those
around you.

It's easy to say, "In God
we trust,"
When life is radiant and fair,
But the test of faith is
only found
When there are burdens to bear.

*When I am afraid, I put my trust
in thee. In God, whose word I
praise, in God I trust without a
fear. What can flesh do to me?*

Psalm 56:3, 4

Today learn to profit from your
losses. It's no big deal to
capitalize on gains … it is
noteworthy to advance after
setbacks.

You can't pluck a rose,
All fragrant with dew,
Without some of its fragrance
Remaining on you.

All the paths of the Lord are
steadfast love and faithfulness,
for those who keep his covenant
and his testimonies.
Psalm 25:10

Today be gentle and kind, and
soon you'll discover that
kindness and gentleness have
become a part of you.

Within the crowded city
Where life is swift and fleet
Do you ever look for Jesus
Upon the busy street?

Hide not thy face from thy
servant ...
Psalm 69:17

Today be assured you are not
alone – the Lord is with you.

Whenever I am troubled
And lost in deep despair,
I bundle all my troubles up
And go to God in prayer.

*He will respond to the prayer of
the destitute; he will not despise
their plea.*

Psalm 102:17 NIV

Today ponder the question,
"What does God want me to do
with my life?"

Teach us, dear God,
That the power of prayer
Is made stronger
By placing the world
in your care!

*When a man's ways please the
Lord, he makes even his enemies
to be at peace with him.*

Proverbs 16:7

Today diminish doubt and
increase your faith.

When someone does
a kindness,
It always seems to me
That's the way God
up in heaven
Would like us all to be.

*Teach me thy way, O Lord, that I
may walk in thy truth; unite my
heart to fear thy name.*

Psalm 86:11

Today let your actions speak
louder than your words. Give
assistance and encouragement to
teachers, principals and
administrators as a new school
term begins.

When life becomes a problem
Much too great for you to bear,
Instead of trying to escape,
Just withdraw in prayer.

The good man does not escape
all troubles – he has them too.
But the Lord helps him in each
and every one …
Psalm 34:19 TLB

Today if you experience a
disappointment, deal with it;
don't let it multiply.

Through a happy springtime
And a summer filled with love,
May we walk into the autumn
With our thoughts
on God above.

*A cheerful heart is a good
medicine, but a downcast spirit
dries up the bones.*
Proverbs 17:22

Today value the beauty of the
changing season. No matter the
time of year there is evidence
that God is near.

God sends His little angels
In many forms and guises,
They come as lovely miracles
That God alone devises.

*Thy hands made me and
fashioned me; give me
understanding, that I may learn
Thy commandments.*

Psalm 119:73 NAS

Today study the lesson of faith,
hope, and love that comes with
the arrival of a "special" child.
Broaden your perspective.
Become a friend to a
handicapped individual.

Take nothing for granted,
For whenever you do,
The joy of enjoying
Is lessened for you.

*Like clouds and wind without
rain is a man who boasts of a
gift he does not give.*
Proverbs 25:14

Today the most memorable
happening will be the one in
which you helped someone else.

Somebody cares and
always will,
The world forgets but God
loves you still.
You cannot go beyond His love
No matter what you're guilty of.

*For thou, O Lord, art good and
forgiving, abounding in
steadfast love to all who call
on thee.*

Psalm 86:5

Today display compassion and
forgiveness, and remember God
forgives you and loves you.

Seasons come and go and with them comes the thought of all the various changes that time in its flight has brought.
But one thing never changes, it remains the same forever, God truly loves His children and He will forsake them never!

Do not hide your face from me, do not turn your servant away in anger; you have been my helper.

Psalm: 27:9 NIV

Today seek ways to encourage the elderly, the middle-aged, or the young in a scholarly or spiritual way.

Prayer is much more
Than just asking for things –
It's the peace and contentment
That quietness brings.

*Lead me in thy truth, and teach
me, for thou art the God of my
salvation; for thee I wait all
the day long.*

Psalm 25:5

Today experience the "prayer"
that resides in your heart. Use
your silent solitude to enrich
your day and to elevate the calm
that is within you.

What will you do
With this day that's so new?
The choice is yours –
God leaves that to you!

This is the day the Lord has made. We will rejoice and be glad in it.
Psalm 118:24 TLB

Today and every day keep your priorities straight – keep first things first.

Let us see in others
Not their little imperfections,
But let us find the good things
That arouse our best affections.

*The beginning of strife is like
letting out water; so quit before
the quarrel breaks out.*
Proverbs 17:14

Today develop the ability to
look for and find Jesus in others.

Meet God in the morning
And go with Him through
the day
And thank Him for His guidance
Each evening when you pray.

*My voice shalt thou hear in the
morning, O Lord: in the
morning will I direct my prayer
unto thee, and will look up.*

Psalm 5:3 KJV

Today join with God early in
the morning and stay in His
company all day and
through the night.

Love works in ways
That are wondrous and strange.
There's nothing in life
That love cannot change.

*A soft answer turns away
wrath, but a harsh word
stirs up anger.*
Proverbs 15:1

Today be an example of agape
love. Be patient, kind, forgiving,
and humble.

It's hard to believe
That God asks no more
Than to bring Him our problems
And then close the door.

The Lord is a stronghold for the
oppressed, a stronghold in times
of trouble. And those who know
thy name put their trust in thee,
for thou, O Lord, hast not
forsaken those who seek thee.

Psalm 9:9, 10

Today trust and obey, and
tomorrow obey and trust.

In trouble and gladness
We can always hear Your voice,
If we listen in silence
And find a reason to rejoice.

*The voice of the LORD is
mighty; the voice of the LORD
is majestic.*

Psalm 29:4 NAB

Today listen for and enjoy the
laughter of children. God is in
their midst.

I have worshipped in churches
and chapels,
I have prayed in the busy street,
I have sought my God and
have found Him
Where the waves of the
ocean beat.

*O come, let us worship and bow
down, let us kneel before the
Lord, our Maker!*
Psalm 95:6

Today, oceanside, countryside,
or mountainside, in a cottage or
in a chalet, know that God is
present when you pray.

Help me when I falter,
Hear me when I pray,
Receive me in Thy kingdom
To dwell with Thee someday.

One thing have I asked of the
Lord, that will I seek after; that I
may dwell in the house of the
Lord all the days of my life, to
behold the beauty of the Lord,
and to inquire in his temple.

Psalm 27:4

Today, if you stumble, know
that God is willing and ready to
assist you to your feet.
Do not fear.

God's love is like a beacon,
Burning bright with faith
and prayer,
And through the changing
scenes of life
We can find a haven there!

*Then they were glad because
they had quiet, and he brought
them to their desired haven.*

Psalm 107:30

Today be an active captain of
your life. Direct your course
toward God's haven. He is your
navigator and your lighthouse.

God is so lavish in all
that He's done
To make this great world such
a wonderful one.
His mountains are high, His
oceans are deep,
And vast and unmeasured the
prairielands sweep.

*In his hand are the depths of the
earth, and the mountain peaks
belong to him.*

Psalm 95:4 NIV

Today admire the artistry of
God: purple mountain peaks,
white-capped oceans of blue,
golden-hued fields of wheat.

God, grant me courage and
hope for every day,
Faith to guide me along my way,
Understanding and wisdom, too,
And grace to accept what life
gives me to do.

*Listen to advice and accept
instruction, that you may gain
wisdom for the future.*

Proverbs 19:20

Today maintain your purpose in
life, act on it, don't just wish for
it to happen. Persevere in your
attempts to achieve your goal.

Give me understanding,
Enough to make me kind,
So I may judge all people
With my heart and not my mind.

He shall judge thy people with
righteousness ...

Psalm 72:2 KJV

Today evaluate the critical
remarks that come your way.
Sort, keep what helps, and throw
the rest away.

The future is not ours to know
And it may never be –
So let us live and give our best
And give it lavishly.

Surely there is a future, and your
hope will not be cut off.
Proverbs 23:18

Today remember that what you
think of yourself is more
important than what others think
of you. You must therefore
think, live, and approve of how
you live.

Father, hear this little prayer,
Reach across the miles from
here to there, so I can feel much
closer to those I'm fondest of and
they may know I think of them
with thankfulness and love.

Answer me when I call, O God ...
Thou hast relieved me in my
distress; be gracious to me and
hear my prayer.

Psalm 4:1 NAS

Today and tonight capture
thoughts of your absent loved
ones. Look through your
scrapbooks and photograph
albums. Pray for them.

Faith is a force that is greater
Than knowledge or power
or skill,
And the darkest defeat turns
to triumph
If we trust in God's wisdom
and will.

Trust in the Lord, and do good;
so you will dwell in the land,
and enjoy security … Commit
your way to the Lord; trust in
him, and he will act.

Psalm 37:3, 5

Today look at the world with a
vision magnified by the power
of faith deep within you.

Do not sit and idly wish for wider, new dimensions where you can put in practice all your good intentions, but at the spot God placed you, begin at once to do little things to brighten up the lives surrounding you.

The path of the righteous is like the light of dawn, which shines brighter and brighter until full day.

Proverbs 4:18

Today concentrate on your God-given talents and use them to help someone.

Dear God, what a comfort to
know that You care
And to know when I seek You,
You will always be there!

*He keeps you from all evil, and
preserves your life. He keeps his
eye upon you as you come and
go, and always guards you.*
Psalm 121:7, 8 TLB

Today knock and seek and
you'll find God waiting for you.
He will console you, soothe you,
and care for you.

Always remember
That whatever betide you,
You are never alone
For God is beside you.

God is our refuge and strength,
a very present help in trouble.
Psalm 46:1

Today be thankful for God's
companionship.